Nothing Works, Everyone Labors

La©luster

Cover Art & Layout design: Mykey Maker / MykeyMadeIt

First Printing
Flint, MI

Contents

Introduction

This collection of poems is the culmination of several years of writing, growth, meditation and revision. Many of these poems appeared in a series of six handmade chapbooks, published between 2011- 2013.

The perspectives captured in this book approach many of the same social problems or physical conditions with very different points of view. Sometimes the perspective is in the first person, to bring the reader into the mind of the narrator. Other times, the reader sees a situation from the outside looking in.

The narrator's emotional states can range from angry and cynical to romantic, hopeful and resilient. Greek heroes and titans occasionally join the cast of characters to offer bits of wisdom on the modern condition and love and lust are juggled like ticking time bombs.

This collection's schizophrenic worldview embodies the constant push and pull of living in a small Rustbelt city where each day is a struggle to decide should I stay or should I go?

I. BURN IT ALL

Go ahead, burn it all but
count on nothing
being changed besides the
ugly peeling paint and
columns of smoke
replacing
pillared skyline shade.

Everything seems more hopeless
as arson artists chisel out a brand new mess
from anger and unhappiness with molten memos
filling demo(lition) lists.

Hate mail, self-addressed,
signed with a gasoline kiss.

If raised sane, ashamed of flaming inheritance.

(If raised sane,) fed up with sordid heroes,
founders and today, all the same,
breaking all our basket eggs into
brownfield stains and live grenades.

No master planning in fifty years
but we're still all slaves.
while
freedom fleas
plague rat race cage.

A brick tide's crashing waves
drown hopes of rehabbed haze. Everything's washed
away
but truth and rage.

So frustrated people set a blaze or pray to escape,
swallowing pride
with deep-seated hate.

This circus city's clowns
joke around with money and lie until it's lost.

Wasting time,
all rundown cogs
in a three-ring broken watch.

Lately though,
I've come to blame idealized fame and a city stripped
of wits by whips, then encouraged to win
a drop out race to bridge card slips.

As descendants of factory fodder,
we inherit mounds of shit and at most, forgetfulness.

Defeatists dealing with
decades of loser rants
and paid off silences.

But our future's not in flames
or at least not yet,
outsourcing's aim
was to discredit
social gains
and pile people with debt.

Now there are two prevailing camps of thought
for living here today-
Either singe away sarcoma homes,
and know in their place
nothing better will ever grow.

Or give up, burn a blunt and
don't worry about changing
what you never cared to really know.

This town's like a dentist's office.
Gummy curbs house holes
where homes were pulled
to save
boxer-tooth blocks
on smiling lanes
from roof decay
and rotting away.

Any second, we could choose
to change the game
and refuse to play
firebomb Monopoly or
pop-off-a-matic Trouble,

but Fly City'd rather
tear itself down
for room to breathe

or live
some dumb fantasy
than

preserve

its rich history
of rubble.

II. GHETTO OF A GIRL

No, no.
You've mistaken my
aimless wanderings
for planned exploration
through the curvy avenues
of your body.

A traveler's wanderlust
where I've carelessly
caressed the gold plaques of your thighs,
thrown bricks through cathedral eyes,
and flicked enough wishing whispers
like stray matches
into your ears to
light the way and hope
you would never feel used.

But you do feel confused.
And worry has been driven
into the dead end streets
across your face.

When all I'm looking for
is a quick place to stub
out this smoldering fame
before my body turns to ash.

You told me to be at home in you
and your asphalt makeup
paved over potholes and gritty
dirt road pasts

but it wasn't enough
to keep my teenage feet
from walking to greener grass.

You may think I
turned your subdivided youth
into a student ghetto
but that wasn't my intention.

And although my drifting
through your city limits was brief,
I've dragged my name and dreams
through wet cement

and spent precious time
pouring a path down your spine-
connecting
your broken heart
to mine.

Like a pale scar,
as a part of you, I'm permanent.

III. HORNY SKIMASK DEMONS

Part 1

(There's a sick hipster
appeal
to living in a
town this real.

There's little here for fun
and home is hell for some who
dip out to craft
big city lives
from the scraps of kings.

The best of us
get hired as escape artists
at age 18.

But there's
no need to blame the evacuees,
they did their time and)

Only god knows what it means...
when most fields in this city
were first
built up dreams, burnt down rapidly
to erase bad memories.

The boom
times are gone and so
is prosperity. The only boom
that makes money
now involves liquor store
robbery and
business is good-

behind weed, greed
and exploitation,
it's the back bone of our
economy.

Heaven's forbid, someone forgive
the need to survive
when no one
provides hope
or a living salary.

Unions established
a false sense
of security but
the ease of
certain things like
summoning cash by smiling
smug sawed-off fangs reminds us
the devil works in mysterious ways
when coping with
desperation and hunger pains, or
if seeking alternatives to
the martyrdom of minimum-wage.

Even with paradise underfoot,
inner demons cause generational pain.

Maybe instead of being the
destitute descendants of opportunity's haze,
perhaps "Horny Skimask Demons"
is a more fitting phrase.

I mean,
isn't that what the headlines read?
Action News spicing up
the verbiage, planting seeds...

And in T.V. times like these,
everybody needs a sacrificial savior
to disrupt the feed
or a monk making
a stand in gasoline for them

to feel at ease
and take the lead.
(But that's not me.)

Fiends seeking
another funeral by fire truck
should crack a beer
and look as
Arson City cashes in on
bad luck and low self-esteem.

Slashed wrists
spewing flames-
delayed results of
fools falling for a
hangman's dream

while leaders drive away
in 4 wheel Ironies,
trailed by folded factories...

Part 2

Stay here long enough and
there's a real chance of getting stuck,
stoned to broke
in a pothole rut.

A looney wolf tricked into
twiddling thumbs
while the trapper comes
instead of gnawing off its
own foot.

Part 3

For a second,
imagine starting over
as the same
kiddy cherubs still
choosing to
chisel wild horns
from woolen halos.

But this time,
let it be enlightening.

This time, as a trusty
corporate angel-
rob the system and earn
yourself a bail out.

Because while everyone agrees that you
should agree to everything when
referred to a pair of split kiss pistol lips,
mouthing SERIOUSNESS
for some dumb
gun metal ventriloquist,

the truth's obvious to
any idiot, that
the security camera
is paparazzi enough
to know you
won't get away with it.

It's funny how many registers
are already stripped down
to their nickels and cents
before the bad guys arrive to
cash out the Coinstar contents.

Corporate crooks still collecting
decades worth of ruinous rents.

Nothing left to steal
except the fillings
from our teeth. So thank god,
mine are made from P.V.C....

Half the population lives up
to polluted expectations
and never leave this shallow sea.

Raised from tadpoles in chlorine fountains,
surviving with deformities.
Waiting to steal kisses from a nonexistent princess
while croaking on modernity.

Possessed with angry notions, the
young trade salvation for a pistol's gleam.

Destined to repeat the cycle,
until hell bound, shot down,
or murderous, rich and free.

End of the day,
we sacrifice ourselves
even though there's
nothing left

besides
vast foundation slabs
like wailing walls
where the temple used to be.

True believers conditioned
to die or live trying,
nothing to do but keep moving and
laugh about this tragedy.

IV. RUIN PORN

Perverts treat posted properties
like prostitutes.

Scrappers are sadists,
prying off
siding
like wrinkled
panties heaped
across slutty truck beds.

Up the street,
exploding houses
surge with horror
and amazement
in the ecstasy of gas-line
fingering.

The Eastside's horny hunger
strokes hard through No Ho Zones,
trading copper for
money shots.

Behind the rain-soaked blinds,
walls have been ripped down
and ravaged
by desperate Johns,
trying to keep up with the Jones'-
drooling over
curled-toe, claw foot tubs
and air ducts forced to give
blow jobs.

A kneeling home's warped wood legs buckle last,
long after her spirit and the front porch.

She condemns herself with Cut/and/Plug mascara,
caked on to distract
from her gutted stare towards
another pimp's hand slapping
FOR SALE BY OWNER
on her ass.

The driveway gets
shaded by lashes of overgrown branches.
The basement trashed
and rancid from former tenants and
cycles of entrapment.
The soul needs to flee
before this coffin gets buried
or smashed in.

Tricks get stripped and teased into foreclosure.
And no one seems to care that this is happening.

So predictably, at childhood's end, ratty
pigtails fray away and
live wires stop sparking-
but fiends will still pay anyway

leaving a busted frame,
barely standing,

and another forgotten address
soon to be erased
from the tax roles. Dead inside,

waiting like a bomb
to be dismantled.

V. DUALING ASTROLOGY

Don't use my birthday
to read the astrology
of our love.

Your
horoscope hopes will wilt away
in search of a fitting name.

I tried to fit the box in July but
my summer stars crowded
the night sky two months
premature,

I bloomed from the dirt
in Spring-
a seeded body
without any roots
to breathe.

I'm some
love child of the moon and seas,
bound to the earth like mud
meant to be tides.

Born early in May,
I crossed the stars
and crowned stubborn horns, refusing
the comfort of anxious claws.

A horny Taurus at heart.
not some tough-shelled crab
boiling under the pressure of being
a person living a double life.

My bullheaded ways
have become cancerous to the ego:

I can't find my place
in the stars and have had
to create my own jacked up constellations.

Being born
in May, doesn't mean I will
be understood by referencing
Mercury in Retrograde and the
way the moon wanes

or that I will become
another one of your predictable
romances, which is one
thing I've never been.

Did the online horoscope tell you we
would need to have this conversation?

Then let's tempt fate and move forward
because I'm seeking
a girl who wants to
know the real me,
not some prophesied Taurus or Cancer-

and definitely not the typical man foreseen
as the Supreme or mistaken as some Misfortune
by one-Dimensional astrology texts.

VI. TRUCK IT UP

Melted vinyl siding resembles
fried egg metaphors when

this is what your block
looks like on the 6 O' clock news
sizzling after some sainted sinner

torched another abando
to keep it vacant of vagrants.

My thanks goes out unsaid to neighbors because
after they sweep away the problems, we
smear the lots with litter. After all these years,
victory is bitter. But
that's not what anyone cares to consider,

desensitized for the next ten months
of their lives with a smug smile

waiting for the city to dig out
the soggy stank of charred timbers.

When they finally do,
they truck it up
and gouge a bigger pit
to sit and wait until shady contractors
get paid and it gets filled in
with trash and dirt and sand.

This is land of the brownfields
and home to the brave.

In mean times
with lifelines drained,
condemned Capitalists
scramble to scrap heavy metals
and feed growing Rock City habits
by dismantling their habitats.

The road to shame
is paved thru a place
of pride and exaggerated danger.
Apathy overtakes anger while
the whole town licks its lips
at the thought of
a wealthy stranger.

Matchstick tempers tend
the flame with cellphone
cameras raised
to catch
a past erased
and the birth
of post-industrial prairie phase.

One hand to press record,
the other hiding cold sweat
above a guilty gaze.

25

Face it, fame is a horrible thing
to strive for because it leaves
room for exploitation and
Youtube video stars
filling channels with their collected
ruin porn.
Sometimes I feel like
it would've been
better to have never been born.

Better than this
anxious existence and
self portrait as scorn.
This city sharpens halos into horns.
Ctrl, alt, arson, mourn.

You see, it's
better for demolitions
to Enter, C/P, delete.

Space.

Better than the truth
we've had to face,
some learn to love.
Others never learn, just live to hate.

VII. EPITAPH (FOR WHEN IT ALL FALLS APART)

I know   you   still love me
                and   maybe knowing
that makes   me   an asshole.

But today, I thought   you
were dead   and
the piece   of   me
that still

cared

finally
died
too.

VIII. VORTEXVILLE

Three expressways in
but no way out.
One way through-
easily confused with
bricks and booze.
Barely a city, first in: bankrupt and underused.

Predictably- we, as citizens,
though few, feel toxic and abused
as ugly factory blues
paint the news with
blood, blight and burnt down schools.
Appealing like road kill
to the flighty New York culture
vultures of cool, who call struggle
quaint and pick at bones like fools.

But the hometown artist
is honor bound to defend his muse
(even from its suicidal self)
and I refuse to let this
refuge for fellow refuse
(otherwise known as Hell)

be scrapped and
collapse from the bulldozer
agendas of
explorers with wealth.

More demolitions everyday
but no one needs
a commune of gated condos
to replace the vacancy
or another exclusive event,
too expensive for locals
to attend while decision
makers devour parcels of
parents' land
like a course
of filets.

So easy to parking lot away great
centurion trees and obvious
opportunities.

So hard to remember
the prosperous city-
all that's left are old curb breaks,
empty union halls
and the Alzheimer's elderly.

Cultivating our
own leaders starts with the
simple seeds of constitutional
literacy because the right to
bear arms is always second to
the number one priority-
respect for others' diversity
and those in the know
know that until now
the country has been
aimed like a plane
on a tragic trajectory.

An epic untold and
 a people polluted with
propaganda imagery.

Now is the time to re-educate ourselves
on what it means to have a sense of humanity, to stand up
and spend a generation
manifesting a new destiny.

IX. ODE TO THE WORKERS OF DELPHI EAST

A pair of yellow signs posted
at different ends of a vast concrete expanse-
One says, "Available: 69- 133 acres, priced to move!"
The other one, advertises
soon to be empty Delphi plants,
"Available: 200,000 to 1,510,000 sq. ft."

This poem is planted in place of a third sign.
The one roadside classified still missing
from that chain link fence,
"Available: a willing work force with bills to pay, families
to feed and nowhere to be..."

Former workers
from other forlorn locals,
sit on their porches,
sipping 40s, remembering when
alarms buzzed them
awake for work on cold sweat mornings.

Making
a living wage,
okay with a tomorrow full of the same,
upward mobility
still a worthy dream... or so it seems

Until fields of plants
were flattened to fit in
an envelope alongside a NAFTA contract, severance
packages
or a wealthy executive's bonus check.

Anymore you'd
assume it was a mirage
if you saw smoky factories
churning out a haze from heavy manufacturing,
now even ghost trains pass thru town unceasingly.
As another major employer
follows the trend.
Mexico-bound
but still headquartered in suburbia,
so sold back to us
not as traitorous
or expatriate

but as American.

X. ODYSSEUS THE NOVELIST
Seeking the muse
at the bottom of a
coffee mug, he only found
sirens in the brown
cliff-like stains
tempting him
to smoke   another
bowl
        and
crash.

XI. GENESEE TOWERS

Towering symbol
of mid-century cement,
soon to be leveled
vacant-vaulted bank in a broke city-
you represent the old paradigm.
Barricaded streets catch
chunks of concrete
falling off facade slabs
basket-woven boxy
across the skyline
…but not for long.
Modernist monstrosity,
the news coverage of your
implosion will not
save you from being
forgotten.
The art deco softness
soon to be
unearthed on the horizon
can't replace your imposing presence
but will give us a chance
to reflect on ourselves differently.
That may be all the spark we need
to ignite a new path, escape the caustic past
and finally rebuild this carved up city
in our own likenesses.

XII. A DAYDREAM

Entering mindless data
on Excel sheets
at his desk, he slipped
into a daydream.
The overhead bulbs and computer screen
unraveled out of focus into blurs of light
like rays of a summer sun.
He felt the warmth of remembered
friends and family camping out

raging until ragged,
happily disheveled in Ohio pastures.
His party years had passed
but he could feel nostalgia's
pull back to the bleary-eyed
music festivals,
the sweaty joy
of a thunderous crowd:
Thousands of revelers
dancing, swaying, drinking,
spaced out under the stars,
loving life into
the late hours of the night.

The tie suddenly seemed taut around his neck.
He wondered if he was killing himself
trying to live like his parents.
He wondered if his new path was purposeless,
if he could ever be himself at work
showing his tattooed flesh
outside the camouflage
of a suit.
He wondered if his
dress shirtsleeves, like an armor
of falsity, were long enough
to hide the inky chainmail draped
across his skin.
Beneath this clean-cut façade,
he thought, is a young life
dangerously well spent
like an archive of state secrets
that must be kept silent.

Whole pictures of a person
aren't meant to fit on a resume.
They're meant to fill a library like Alexandria
and then when time comes for change,

adulthood begins
with the past
burnt away.

XIII. GENESEE TOWERS (POST-IMPLOSION REMIX)

Towering symbol- of what? I forget.

Vacant-vaulted bank in a broke city,
you represent the old paradigm.

For years,
barricaded streets caught chunks of concrete
falling off facade slabs
basket-woven boxy across the skyline...
but no longer.

Like you,
our insides felt laced
with red tape and blasting caps.

Like you,
we were sneered at,
reviled.

Like you,
we've been built up
just to get torn down.

Modernist monstrosity
lying in a heap,
even though we can replay
your death from every angle

and will be plucking pink insulation
guts from tree branches
until Spring-

the news coverage of your
implosion will not
save you from being
forgotten…

After the last truckload is hauled away,
the art deco softness
unearthed on the horizon

will not replace your imposing presence
but will give us room to breathe and maybe that's
all the spark we need to ignite a new path and
finally rebuild this carved up city
in our own likenesses.

XIV. SISYPHUS PUSHING PAPER
Voted "most likely to succeed" and high school prom king,
Sisyphus is pushing paper in a dead end job
60 hours a week
to afford rent in a
luxury building, and 600 square feet.
His efforts fulfilled with a rising career but
too busy paying bills to appreciate the view
except in too short forgotten dreams

before the
alarm,
the alarm, the alarm, th-
wakes him from wondrous sleep.
Hell is a high rise in a fancy city
and no one to share the view with.
Cursed is being chained to a desk and a meager paycheck
wondering what happened to your life
between the pale knives of
florescent
lights and
your
last breath…

XV. ODE TO LOWELL JR. HIGH

I remember
when my cub scout troupe
sat on the concrete stoop
behind the school
carving Jack-o-lanterns for Halloween.
Mounds of orange flesh scooped
onto the grass,
a pulpy model of the auto parts yards
over the fence next door.
Not so many years later, in need of a scrap yard part,
I drive past what's left
of the old Franklin Avenue business district.
Craterous brick-lined puddles
moldering in the rain.
Driving past the tall grass and blackened trees,
past curb brakes leading to
new found fields with street names.

Lowell, vacant for a few years now, is
adorned with graffiti flourishes and boarded windows,
gouged out and gruesome looking.
A towering smoke stack,
without the foliage of a furnace,
still stands like a petrified stump
clear cut in the forests of forgotten
industries.
This school's present includes its insides
smashed for quick cash like a mineral resource.
Education, these days is less of a priority
than the destructive
dismantling of this aging community.
A late November refugee
from a rain-streaked Halloween,
the school still stands but sadder looking now
with a frost-bitten pumpkin's meatless lean.
The only place this school still vibrantly exists
is in its former students' photographs and memories.

Even a few years can be too long for an asset to sit.
And the only question
anyone thinks to ask isn't,
how can we learn from the past?
But how much longer
before they demolish that thing?

XVI. THANKS FOR SHOOTING SPOONFULS

Thanks for shooting up spoonfuls of stars
into the black hole veins of your spiral arm galaxy.

Since energy can't be created nor
destroyed, I hope you continue
to waste away- shoveling bad energy out
of the way for others choosing a
much brighter path.

I agree, there is
a narcotic warmth to the
burnt space rock ritual,
which you first likened to devouring
suns whole.

But no, you are not a hero.

Just a planet losing its atmosphere.

One tribe too ignorant to see the
ruin lurking behind their own volcanic gods.

Your meteoric habit, on the outside looking in,
is just a desperate search
for occasional small flares

to break up the nothingness
of your own
clouded night sky…

and soon,
there won't be anyone left to keep searching.

XVII. SAD ARSON HEARTS

I only go for girls
with dry wit
and sad arson hearts.

The ones I date
lick lips, dragging
Zippo clicks across
their chests, playfully
threatening to go
through with it.

I'm a fool…
I'm a fool for that, just
a product of my environment.

I'm not into girls
that nibble on their
fingertips, determined
to sit because
the future's stamped
with hopelessness.

No, I'm down with
the defiant chicks
that phoenix out
when faced with
foreclosure or having
their copper dresses
stripped.

I've learned not
all of us can be fixed but
I'm stuck on girls that repossess their own
destinies
even if that means the
whole
squatting-inferno-Juliet-Romeo-
poison-dagger-
thing.

I've spent dizzying nights
with girls who
giggle about their
crumbling lipstick architecture
and the bitter
Michigan weather.

Wondering if a little fire
will bring them clarity.

As a kid, I dreamt about fixing
the derelict buildings of my
Midwestern city. All of which
have since been erased
by fire, work crews and misery.

I knew nothing about C/Ps or girls and less
about the real world.

But I've known
the sharp pain of heartbreak and disappointment
well enough by now, that it barely phases me.

Sometimes
you have to sacrifice
a house full of dreams to
find your real home even

if that means,
setting up camp on a
patch of new grass
and re-imagining.

XVIII. BROKE

"But we will never be broke,"
she said.

"Because we are wealthy
in spirit. We have
stockpiles of pride
and chests full of hope.

"They will have to
build bigger jails to
house
our hearts or begin
taxing happiness
because we refuse
to play the fugitive
sending rich dreams
on the lam.

"We refuse
to be outlaw kings and
queens trying to bury
those shining treasures
under triple Xs."

She said, "Wear your crown jewels
wild and free,"

And a little older now, I
can sorta' see.

Cash poor, I still manage to pay the bills
in filigree.

Self-confidence
being the gold-tooth secret to
mastering alchemy.

XIX. BULLDOZER AND HIS BUNGALOW

Lover, I want to rip into you
like a demo crew
with a passion for
their jobs.

I want to film our
smash session,
and tenderly label it "Ruin Porn."

Babe, I wanna be the Bulldozer
to your boarded up Bungalow.

I want to plow your lovely ashes,
torched by callous assholes,
into your open basement.

I want you to see yourself
not as they have made you,
but as a clearer sunset,
non-existent and naked,

a horizon line
not yet redefined but no longer dwelling
on your flaws or feeling
like a wasteland.

I want to be the one
who takes you off the grid.
I want to sweep you
off your feet.

I know you think
your heart has been stolen
by metal thieves
mining through the drywall.

But I'm not here looking to remodel,

I'm here to make you crumple
into sheets.

I'll haul out
the debris of your esteem
by hand if I have to,

thrust truckloads of soil in its place,
exhaling diesel breath heat.

Soon
we'll spoon,
having had our fill,

sod and straw strewn
like tidal waves to wash away
a past life's pain
and
help you rest in peace,

somewhat whole again

instead of forsaken forever,
condemned
by your
self-defeating,
                    soul-destructive
                                    loneliness.

XX. MOST DANGEROUS FAME
PART 1. Situational Comedy

The indigenous are endangered
and the sprawl is known
to swallow strangers like a jungle.
With forked tongues,
guerillas gather
on porch-lit stages
scheming to
feed the struggle.
Respect rarely beats paid praises-
Not to pop the bubble, but
talent is wasted.

Poverty's hyped as True Life
when a "steady job"
involves selling hazes.

Born shivering with
thick-skinned coat of pride,
a hide stolen by
skinny-gened racists.

Primal chic
as destructive as invasives.

Tattooed with assuming gazes,
hip poachers from the "mainland"
defined a preserved wasteland
out of our brick-lain stable.
Pacifying kids in cages, drugged and bobbing,
hooked by lines of cable.

Sidewalk cafes, serving status,
from the safety
of reserved tables.
Dominion dismantled, judged lacking
in all but labels.
As game, we live in haste and
evolve when we are able.
Reclaiming cracks in pavement,
using fame to feed the struggle-
blaming Systematic Hustle
but the truth is only mumbled.

No one expects you to save us,
credit card chance of a dream-
scrap pipes to make payments.

Think "rumble,"
not "flight,"- invest in confidence,
bank on true statements.
If you catch my drift,
you cannot fumble.

Paychecks
can pay for life's phases,
but the change is only
subtle.
We're workhorses reborn
feral, surviving
(the dead of night)-
silent, foaming careful.
See'in new dreams
from all new sides
without the blinding
straight and narrow.

You Are Here, fight
to rewrite maps and
draw new arrows.
The rotten power lines
vine, tower and climb
above those who tripped and tumbled,
above space(d out) heater huddles.
The change is only subtle.
Brick meadows bloom with
grit and grime, abando forests
house street names and rubble.

Half the town's been
burnt alive but it only
feeds the struggle.

PART 2. Declaration of Survival

Born to blame the Systematic Hustle,
born test rats for Electric Haterade
and institutions bound
to crumble.
A habitat designed
for breeding lowlife scum
and trouble. High-rise buildings
taken as trophies,
ashen children forced
to stumble.
And the sidewalk cracks
are getting bigger as
more spirits haunt
the trigger, as the victims
clutch their fingers,
fearful of the neighbor.
Nothing works,
Everyone labors.

The stabber hunted
daybreak in darkness,
on safari for hope
and swagger.

We're
wildlife to them, beasts,
once tame, now
lame or haggard.

The herd's thinned out
and staggered but these predators
can be captured. Venom-less snakes,
their fables keep them raptured.
They pray in grassy chapels.
We, prey, eat only
apples. But they're fermented
in a tonic and we
live drunk off of
the knowledge, sloshed under
the moon- happy, howling.
"Coo-coo-ka-choo, my
pelt looks like this,
but scowling!"
Your eyes are bejeweled,
hollow points
squeezed by ivory rings.

Blood on your shoes- young bucks, like me,
with horns removed, egos bruised.
The hunted, desperate, learn to see.
The hungry, fed up, yearn to feed.

PART 3.   No Tax Base to Taxidermy

Decay's got a lively following. Slop
up tourist pigs and slather meatless ribs,
gravy-gasping, butchered, wallowing.

Cavities in the K-9s. Arrogance, like
Pride, out prowling.

Leaving lasting legacies
deliberate with depravity.

Dead-eyed decoys, strung up by gravity-
Pendulums in the clockwork, running out of time.
Children mean mug the sun for shine,
regression gnawing on the spine.

Epitomize unraveling because
bitter grapes make better wine.
Instead of orange vests,
hunters dress to impress in
saggy pants, stick-poke tats,
diamond stings.

Their stylish fakes of kicks and hats
lure cougar cats and vultures, bait for
festering rats who
dine on bling.
News of sweat's deluge
will wash away kongs and kings.
Tidal tourist splash displaces
more than fiends and trash.

Shoot camera flash to capture
the speed of broken glass.
It's shuttering.

'magination makes mansions
out of dens of crack,
explorers' awe intact, bewildered, stuttering:
"P-P-Politcal correctness makes this
mess less cluttering." Raise standards, not rent-
a toast to no bread
and all buttering.

Salvage the subliminal. A savage isn't simple.
Forage for a bigger grimace and fangs
dropped below the dimples.

Replenished as a cotton crop.
Stillborn in a chill spot,
Stuck on the scent
of supple suggestions and why not?
Upstage the
contingent of contagion
with the
legion of lepers.
Don't confuse speculators
with spectators.
Climb the
scaffolding of scandals.

Survive the ordeal for ideals,
dig digital depictions as myths,

plight as pleasure,
ragged as rugged,

the margins as maternal.

The dirt's fitter here,
fertile.
Mother's milk, sickly,
curdled.

We wolves wrapped in lamb's skin,
chaos carnal, post-bust,
pre-maturely came,
mounted, romanticized, nutty,
unnamed.
Bred rough around the edginess,
and still most dangerous
at this game.

XXI. FACELESS PEARL

Another faceless girl perched
at the end of the bed
cooing daybreak under
my eyelids.

Posed nude with neck
outstretched like a hen
hungry to be plucked again
or a strange interpretation
of an Italian flamingo
taken from some fashion magazine
to disguise her insecurities.

Feathered eyes looking ahead
in time to after our
eventual grind and passionate fry,
beyond the choice of
feast on breast meat
or dine on her spine,
to where we recline

her heart nested
next to mine,

slipping away
back to sleep for a few
hours before she decides
its time to finally fly.

XXII. ALL MY FRIENDS

All my friends
are up to their eyeballs
in tattoos. They all rock backpacks
even though some of them haven't been in school
for a decade.
Most ride bikes or did or
would if it wasn't so cold 5 months a year.
These friends are as comfortable
crowded on a smoky sidewalk outside the bar

as they are at the Point
off Island Street, overlooking the
river's concrete banks as
sunsets crash molten red
into the paved-over brownfields.
Ghostly whispers wander
the old jobsite   carried
on the breath of the wind
and we add our whiskey-slick
exuberance
and graffiti-tongued bliss to the mix
like we're kids again.

All my friends (or at least
the ones I find worth keeping near)
understand the appeal
of a cheap house with a side lot
and a scraggly
sweat-built food forest
that won't produce for four more lean years.
If I don't say so myself,
all my friends are cool cats or rude
dogs or phamily freeks
hunting down
enough loot to make a new start...
or at least a partial payment
to avoid the shut off notices

for another month.

XXIII. HOMETOWN POEM (NO RUSH)

Lawns plastered with signs
fighting to be seen:

"For sale," "For lease." "Rent to own,"
"First month free."

In my hometown,
there's so many choices on
which place to be.

In my head,
there's just one life to live
i.e. to flee
but fortunately, for me,
there's no rush.

The city cemeteries are lush and
might as well blink neon lights
reading VACANCY.

The car may have raised and razed
Buick City but the irony
is killing me.

While all the basement Buddhists meditate
under bloom-cycle lights, making bucks,
growing Kush, thinking deeply about their own suffering.

A generation of garbage pail kids,
born with a broom in hand
to clean up ancestral debris.

A place where 8 people per day give up
and move away worry free.

They can't see anything left to save
just a broken tribe in an oil stain.

And the sad part is, they aren't far off...

Staying here is more of a burden
than a point of pride

or at least for the longest time,
that's how things felt to me

because despite whatever happy face
I want to feign,
or injustice
I could lock my door and ignore
instead of stress to change-
there's just
not much still standing
that deserves the praise:

a few
pillared rows of half-burnt,
gutless homes,

chess piece-
investment groves played out
in Downtown revival zones,

and a few well hidden
hornets' hives
where gaunt artists thrive
in a daze
haunting the flower fields
of their minds.

A little buzzed,
they spit spun out poetic phrase. Softly
composing cracks of lightning
that lead to thunderous refrains.

Jaws rattling ferocious behind snake-bite fangs,
hissing anti-venom spit, a mumbled rattle
sub-wolfed into a wild howl
penetrating the unknown like
lapping licks of an
inner shiver craze.

These impassioned
kids make clunky claims to fame
even though no one will ever know their name.

Lives comparable to
an upshot drop of water
from a sprinkler
sputtering
as background noise
to the pouring rain.

Pilgrims to the pillage,
they're drawn here and have stayed.

So I'll do the same
until the roof caves in
or my motivation dissipates

like smoke clearing
from throwing ink at
expectations,

throwing out poems like
pin-pulled grenades.

©
©
©
©
©
©

La©luster

THINGS SEEM DARK IN THIS PIT OF VIPERS
BUT THERE'S STILL TIME TO CHANGE.

SHED YOUR SKIN,
WASTELANDIA

TOMORROW IS A
BRIGHTER
DAY.

GLOSSARY

C/P:
Cut and plugged, letters spray-painted on abandoned houses by utility workers when gas and water lines been shut off in preparation for demolition. This prevents the structure from unintentionally exploding.

Scrapping:
The act of procuring and selling secondary metal products, such as copper pipes, aluminum siding or other desirable metals, to scrap yards for a profit.

Ruin Porn:
Phrase describing exploitative media documenting decaying architecture and vacant spaces.

No Ho Zones:
Phrase written on neighborhood signs as signal to prostitutes and "johns" that neighbors won't tolerate their presence.

The Stabber:
Reference to Elias Abuelazam, a man convicted of 18 counts of stabbing attacks in 2010, primarily of elderly black men in Flint. Known as the Genesee County Serial Stabber.

NAFTA:
Acronym for North American Free Trade Act

ACKNOWLEDGMENTS

Acknowledgement is made to the following publications for versions of these poems which originally appeared in them.

Qua: "Burn it All," "Sad Arson Hearts," "Vortexville," "Thanks for Shooting Spoonfuls," "All my Friends," "Hometown Poem (No Rush)"
The Offbeat: "Ghetto of a Girl," "Faceless Pearl"
Red Fez: "Horny Skimask Demons part 1 and 2"

The author would also like to thank all of the editors, muses and collaborators who helped shape this collection. Without their contributions, this book would be a puddle of ink stillborn in a printer cartridge. No contribution is small, every eye, ear and eloquent critique is appreciated.

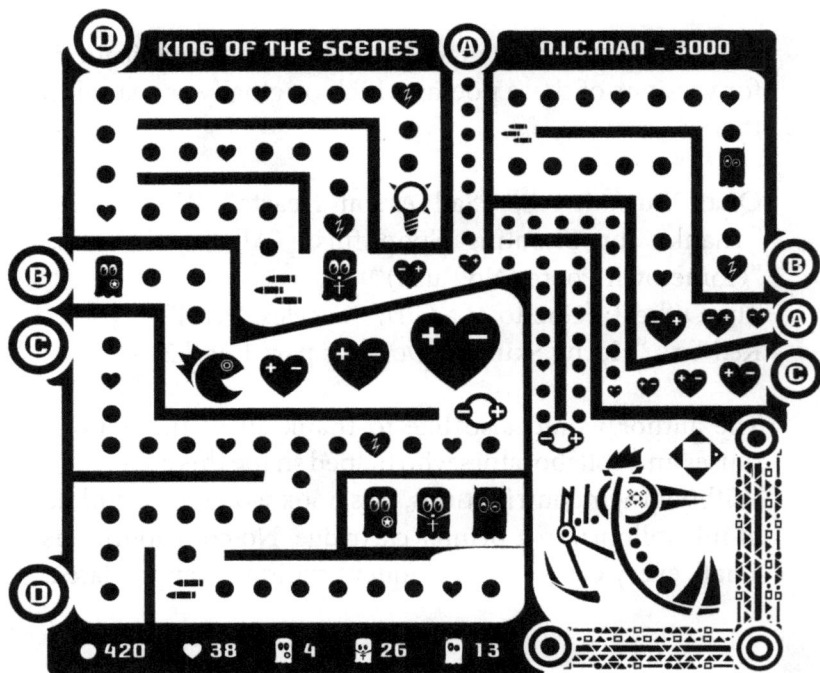

KING OF THE SCENES • N.I.C.MAN - 3000

● 420   ♥ 38   4   26   13

Shoegazing stargazers
are nodding off with
dusted eyes and
smiling down
upon themselves
in this early morning fix

* 9 7 8 0 6 9 2 4 3 4 9 0 1 *